Belinda Rimmer

Touching Sharks
in Monaco

Indigo Dreams Publishing

First Edition: Touching Sharks in Monaco
First published in Great Britain in 2019 by:
Indigo Dreams Publishing
24, Forest Houses
Cookworthy Moor
Halwill
Beaworthy
Devon
EX21 5UU

www.indigodreams.co.uk

Belinda Rimmer has asserted her right under the Copyright, Designs and Patents Act 1988 to be identified as the author of this work.

ISBN 978-1-912876-08-2

British Library Cataloguing in Publication Data. A CIP record for this book can be obtained from the British Library.

Designed and typeset in Palatino Linotype by Indigo Dreams.
Cover design by Ronnie Goodyer at Indigo Dreams
Printed and bound in Great Britain by 4edge Ltd.

Papers used by Indigo Dreams are recyclable products made from wood grown in sustainable forests following the guidance of the Forest Stewardship Council.

For my sons, Sam and Pete, with much love

Acknowledgements

Thank you to Diana Taylor for awarding, *water*, first prize in the Cheltenham Poetry Festival's 2017 Poetry in Motion Competition; to Roy McFarlane for selecting, *Scoot*, as a runner up in the 2017 Gloucestershire Writers Network Competition; and to Malika Booker for placing, *Sapling*, second in the Ambit Poetry Competition, 2018.

My thanks also go to the following editors of magazines and webzines in which some of these poems first appeared: *Ink Sweat & Tears, Confluence, Foxglove, Eye Flash, The Poetry Village, Atrium, Under the Radar, Pulsar, The Poetry Shed* and *Ambit*.

A special thank you to Jennie Farley for her patience, support and mentoring; to Anna Saunders for all she does for Cheltenham poetry; to Cheltenham Poetry Society for their ongoing encouragement; and to my Charlton Kings poetry group, such a warm environment to try things out under the guidance of Angela France. Last, but not least, thank you to Ronnie Goodyer and Dawn Bauling for helping so many poets to realise their dreams.

CONTENTS

water

when i become water
i shall be a lake full of fish and stone
        upon me wooden boats will bob
    children in bobble hats
will row my perimeter
or across to my island –
almost too far to see from land –
to swing on rope   climb trees   outpace horses

you'll know me

i shall be friendly and let each gaze
touch my honest surface
                i won't be in a hurry
i'll dawdle

animals will come to drink from me
locals wrapped in goose-fat will swim my laps
or sit in deckchairs on grassy banks to read books

in spring and summer
belted kingfishers will build
nests   they'll choose the side in the sun

once   before rivers ran dry
and oceans died   when the sky held rain
there were many lakes

swirling and fertile and deep
                but i will be the only one
        when i become water

Sixpence Purse

I think the blood came from my mother's finger
as she fumbled to secure her buttonhole.

I know she carried this purse
on her wedding day – inside a sixpence, a talisman.

I keep it in a matchbox. Only I get to touch
its cracked cream leather and delicate clasp.

Everything, the little stitches, white popper
and lucky sixpence, speaks of my mother.

I'd sneak into her room, let that purse transform me
from awkward girl into bride.

Swishing up the aisle in my puff-ball dress
I'd see it

all before me – a husband, two children, a dog,
promise of a family life.

Brittle

She ran the last bit as she always did,
turning at the edge of the wood, kicking
up clumps of moss, ready to jump.

She crouched. In a moment of release she leapt,
lightly lifting her bones, feeling the freedom of it.
The ditch seemed to welcome her –

the nettles in their bed of green,
lazy white flowers slumping to-and-fro.
She emerged on wobbly legs. Skin blistered, eyes wide.

She had to do it again from the other side,
gathering enough pace to pitch clear but letting herself drop.
Nothing else had touched her this way.

Afterwards, she dipped her arms into a cooling stream,
pain dissolving in a spray of late spring.

Scoot

Made from long forgotten toys and bike bits,
my scooter arrived on the doorstep, big and clumsy.
My father hoped scooting would put meat on my bones.
I got the hang of it straight away.
I'd clatter down kerbs, flatten daisies
and criss-cross empty roads. Sometimes
I'd carry foot passengers, mostly teddies
or an occasional obliging cat.
In the rain my scooter cried blood –
trickles of red paint and rust.
No one coveted my wonky pram wheels,
chewed rubber handles and tinny bell.
For years I scooted along
not caring if skin peeled from elbows,
stones embedded into knees
or bubble wrap blisters appeared on palms.
I had the means to go between
the fields and the estate, the shops and the subway,
my house and friends. And to go alone.
My father would watch from the window,
hands either side of his head in defeat.
However hard I scooted
I still wore my bones.

Drift

Snow on the ground, patches of green forewarn a slow melt –
no white Christmas. Eager for another ride before snow turns
to slush, my son has stopped mid-sledge to pose for a picture.
I hunker down beside him. My arm rests across his knee,
easy, natural. I'm wearing pink wool – hat, scarf, mittens –
and heavy boots. Our eyes squint into a low sun. We smile
in different directions. Beyond the picture – cups of cocoa,
slippery chips, stars in a darkening sky and an icy path home.

The lake already frozen, leaves like shark fins pushing through
the ice. Different this year, the house now empty –
my boys out in the world. Stacking clouds promise a storm,
maybe early snow. A robin settles, tiny under winter feathers.
I was trying so hard not to think of Christmas.

Between the branches enough mistletoe to decorate the doors.
I reach, no longer ballerina-elegant. I still believe in kissing
under mistletoe. What would it be like to kiss a stranger?
What taste? What wayward tongues?

Orchard

No more greenfinch,
no more treecreeper,
no more sparrow hawk;

hedgerows slashed
to make way for roads.
Orchards torn up for houses –

confused woodpeckers
still seek dead-wood and bug.

On a single patch of grass
in the midst of brick and slate
two apple trees remain.

One scarred black as dried blood,
the other, gnarly eyed
for staring into windows.

Pom-poms

Shades of red, green, gold, like Christmas baubles
or fairy lights. My mother's basket of wool.
She began to knit, needles click-clacking,
neat stitches in shades of red, green, gold.

Scarf, shawl, blanket?
Soft parcel of dolls clothes?
My task, to hold the wool high,
face turned to the pom-poms of her tartan slippers.

One evening after *Coronation Street*
my mother let out a growl
where a growl shouldn't be –
speared by a needle.

My mouth formed an 'O'
and drew in air to swallow the growl.
I put my hands on her back.
She smelled of flowers.

I wanted to kiss her, to hold her in the crook of my arm,
to keep touching, touching, touching.
Like King Arthur's sword in the stone,
I pulled, and pulled the needle free.

My mother smiled at me
as if she often smiled at me.
She took up her knitting.
I took up the wool, my face turned

to the pom-poms of her tartan slippers.

Saturday Job

Service station grease,
travellers scoffing chips and burgers, warm lemonade.
A low sun crawling through smeared windows.

It's nowhere near end of shift.
I vacuum the aisles,
drown in my own thoughts –

bovver boys, Bowie on repeat,
a dead badger at the side of the road.

The supervisor groans
and grabs the Hoover. It sucks
as if sucking a sun from the sky.

I squirm inside my ill-fitting body,
feel a bud of breast against overall.

On the bus home we Saturday girls
talk endlessly about our bodies.
Some of us already bleed.

We fall silent
to honour the badger,
dead at the side of the road.

To Alison

We'd often stop off on the way back from work in some sleazy bar where no one knew us. You drank pints of lager like the boys. We played penny slot machines, fed the jukebox, Joan Armatrading or Dylan. Sometimes we'd go to your flat to carry on drinking. Displayed on a table, photographs of you modelling on a beach. You said you weren't as pretty as you'd once been. I found your eyes beautiful with their black centres, or courageous. When we touched, our skins blurred and burned. We were young, not yet adults, and this was new, unusual, exposing. It happened on a sharp bend, you in a hurry in the leaves and rain. I thought then of those sleazy bars and the way our skins had blurred and burned.

Daffodils

The day Anthony Minghella died
I stitched myself into a chair to watch *Truly, Madly, Deeply*
on repeat – with the grainy softness of video
and a supply of cotton hankies.

My empathy always with Nina, hurting so hard
she couldn't let go, and no one knowing the right thing to say.
Jamie's ghost wasn't enough. He came back in the wrong way,
as ghosts are prone to do, with his mess and musty smell.

I picked a bunch of daffodils to remember Minghella,
brought them inside to set centre table,
glad it wasn't summer with roses and carnations.

Almost eight years later,
the car radio told me Alan Rickman had died.
I pulled off the road, longing to hear Jamie's ghost,
maybe a favourite line from *Truly, Madly, Deeply*.

Nothing.
I thought, no one dies properly.

I picked a bunch of daffodils to remember Rickman,
brought them inside to set centre table,
glad it wasn't summer with roses and carnations.

She Flies Like a Bird

Grandpa fetches a bowl of pea pods.
She runs her thumbnail along each crease
releasing pale peas onto the path.

She nudges them with a toe – green, green against grey.
The peas seem to sing up at her, *eat me, eat me.*
She prefers jelly.

No new shoes until her legs fill out,
no dancing dresses, no crimson socks.
But soon she'll be slimmer than the lady in the balloon
drifting above the clouds with her slice of nimble.

She's a kid and determined to keep it that way.
Bones, lean as crispy bacon.
She follows Grandpa to his allotment where tomatoes cluster

and marrows like carbuncles litter the soil.
He throws her a spud. She lifts it to the sun,
sees it from the inside out, all pink veined.

Better these fresh veggies, Grandpa says,
than all the jelly in the sea.

Belly Button

On nights so dark I think of eclipses,
my fingers ache from probing.
I am trying to find a fragment of my mother
inside my belly button.

One small discovery and we could be reconciled.

Hours with only fluff and other debris to show.
My belly feels sore, tight.
Nothing prepares me for a seahorse.

A bloody seahorse, stuck part way out, tail hooked.
I ease it onto my chest.
It bobs about happily in a bowl of salty water.

What is it trying to tell me?

To forget the whole nurturing business,
focus on making my own way as his kind must do,
or get what I need from books –
there are plenty of good mothers (and fathers) lurking
within the pages.

Note: *Male seahorses give birth; neither parent care for their young.*

Hide

Snipes have long beaks, he says. *Long beaks*
to feel for worms. They know exactly where to look.
Like you or me reaching under the bed for our slippers.

I ready my camera.
I don't own any slippers.

Lapwings, he says, *are also called green plovers*
or peewits because of their call.

I zoom-in, focus.
Then I hear it – Pee-wit. Pee-wit.

I turn to him as if he's unlocked a great mystery,
stay listening as birders leave the hide.

He could tell me everything, he says, *about estuary birds.*
But I am still unravelling that perfect sound.

Later, I imagine him reaching for his slippers,
hands curling around in the dark.

Road Kill

It hung from the garage rafters by its feet,
the pheasant my father had run over
on the way out of Partridge Green.

For many nights after
I thought only of that bird –
the strange angle of its neck,
its staring eyes
and the crescent of blood on the garage floor.

When I found my mother plucking feathers –
bloody intestines in the bottom of the bin
and a sticky aroma of death –
I ran away to the fields at the back of our house

to watch the birds in flight,
wings gleaming in the sun.

Born of Birds

I suited the science of jumping.

For years, plimsoll shod, I'd leap through the air,
land bottom-up in the midst of a stormy sandpit.

I won medals, courted crowds
who shouted my name with trumpet breath.

I believed in everlasting childhood,
hated the dull hunched ache of breasts.

They threw me off kilter –
no more hop, skip, jump.

In dreams I'm often perched in trees –
a tribute to that time

when I was born of birds.

Stationary Traveller

A photograph ripped from a travel book
lives above my kitchen sink, away from the sun.
It's an Arctic polar night –
aurora flashes, snow on the hills, a lake,
a single fishing boat, a smattering of cottages –
familiar as the way my hair curls in humidity.
I don't want this trip,
rallying against endless dark.
Some tour guide, whiff of fish,
cruel change in the weather would spoil
the ringing silence, deep beauty, perfect balance.
It's a geography of routine places me in my kitchen
wearing a Nordic moment like an apron,
tied tight at the waist,
every time I wash the dishes.

Salute

On a boat to America.

She's downy as a cat
with feline vision,

sees the sorry looks
of the other passengers
at how she carries her bones.

In New York

she'll drop
her prognosis in the Hudson,

stroll through Central Park
to immerse herself in languages
she has no ear for
but touch her just the same,

and catch the Staten Island ferry
to salute Lady Liberty.

She'll send a postcard home:
in New York. I am alive.

Circle in a Spiral

Squashed inside the shed,
six of us – *The Invited.*

Our club is in full swing.
We're up to our tricks,
pin-pricked skin: *Blood Sisters.*

Cigarettes from my mother's pack
lined up like *Snow-Queen* fingers
alongside a bottle of lemonade laced with gin.

Rat-a-tat on the door.

My father's voice,
crab-apple sharp.
Where's Paul?

Pins and blood-soaked tissues
shoved into an empty plant pot.
Inside my sleeve tobacco tendrils.

Only my brother has my father's attention.
Are we holding a secret,
hiding Paul?

He's found at once
in the neighbour's garden
lost in a game of make-believe.

For a moment
I imagine myself   missing –

Stolen

He was behind me,
an uncomfortable draft
as if a door had sprung a leak.
A flash of movement,
hands lifting my skirt –
blue and bought from Chelsea Girl.
A stolen look at my knickers
and fourteen year old legs
dotted with disco-ball light.
I've never quite forgotten it –
an uncomfortable draft
as if a door had sprung a leak;
a wedge of exposure, a theft.

F Word

It fell
from my lips like a little devil,

bloodied and hot,
scuffing the rainy pavement.

It was speak up
or never speak again.

He chased me to the end of our road,
gave me what-for.

I breathed the word over and over,
knowing it would transcend everything.

I often think of that day,
the rain spilling, my father's hand upraised,

that word
coming between us.

Glare

No forwarding address,
just a note – Gone to Australia –
and a book, *Girl in a Swing.*
Inside, an inscription: *Read into this? With love.*

A pain, low in my abdomen,
something sick and grumbling.

I'd driven him away. I was hard things.
Stone. Wood. Too silent.
Left him to ache in the dark hours,
couldn't give him a snug place.

Decades on, the book is unread.
I often thumb the delicate pages until everything intensifies.
It still hurts,
the way eyes hurt in the sun.

Swap

I had not reckoned on this arrangement,
a swap – the wife and you, me and the husband.
I floated about their house, tried to get lost in different drinks.
You had set it up – me and the husband, you and the wife.
I was not to have a say.
I was in the husband's bedroom.
His wife's nightdress on the pillow.
The husband's breath quickened and I felt like
I didn't want to, not with him,
not with his wife's nightdress on the pillow.
No means no, I said.

No means no, I said.
Not with his wife's nightdress on the pillow.
The husband's breath quickened and I felt like
I didn't want to, not with him,
his wife's nightdress on the pillow.
I was in the husband's bedroom.
I was not to have a say.
You had set it up – me and the husband, you and the wife.
I floated about their house, tried to get lost in different drinks.
A swap – the wife and you, me and the husband.
I had not reckoned on this arrangement.

Touching Sharks in Monaco

Through the skylight a rectangle of grey
hints at thunder. Around the touch tank
children in bright cottons, chattering. I shush them.

Our guide demonstrates –
safe ways to touch, the need for care – in three languages.

I'm drifting back to Brighton –
bum bouncing on a plastic chair,
distant splash of dolphin and whale.
Clearly, Monaco knows how to do aquariums.

Sleeves rolled up, I'm here for the shark.
I probe the tank's cool salty water.
He glitters, bumps the walls, and turns.
It's all or nothing, now or never.

I slide my hand deeper.
He's sandpaper rough against my open palm.

Someone shouts, *Stop!*
I've forgotten everything:
the two finger rule, how to stroke a dorsal fin.

The shark escapes to the other side,
to children with thumbs and spare fingers neatly tucked away.

She calls across the tank, *just remember for next time.*
Our guide, so certain of my return.

Blades

She flipped the knives in the drawer,
covered them with a tea towel.

Her son knew nothing of her fear.
How she imagined
her hand slipping to pierce
his little heart
under chubby white skin,
smug with newness.

If his hair fell into knots
she didn't untangle it,
afraid one small hurt
could lead to another.

To soothe him she played
Beethoven in the front room
away from those sharp edges.

She scratched his name
into the wooden window frame,
a talisman. Still those knives
haunted her, day and night,
an unvoiced shadow.

Acrobat

Down slippery slopes
drenched in summer-drizzle
two boys are racing.

The youngest out-running his brother
until, like a circus acrobat
caught double somersault,

he flies through the air,
lands in a perfect squat.
Ahead, silhouetted against the vines,

his older brother raises his arms in victory –
the distance between them
like a lost chance.

Summer's End

At summer's end we came to race boats
across the ford at Kineton.

We carried nets, Thermos flasks,
wore red to deter wasps.

Today the valley thrums with insects.
Ants like magnetic particles drawn to the surface,
I tread them back into the earth.

Vulnerable to drought
the ford is a cobble-stoned puddle.
Silt will slow its journey to the Thames.

No sound, no trickle, no gush.

Two horses gallop over –
a faint smell of grass and peppermint –
then shy away.

In this moment of birdsong,
ox-eye daisies and variegated light,
it's the way someone has fixed the rotten gate
with blue twine that captures me.

This one thing –
the impermanence of wood.

Gloucester Docks

She ripples like an iris, outshines the sun.
She's waving leaflets and chanting,
Jesus loves you; put your trust in Jesus.

At the dockside café I stare into my coffee.
She streams over, in her wake an orange afterglow.
I choke on my cake, push away from my chair.

She thrusts a leaflet under my nose, *Are You a Good Person?*
Every passer-by seems to turn to me.
I think of all that has gone, of all I have done.

She skirts the shadowed edges of tall ships,
vanishes into the pink-skinned, flip-flopped crowd,
words echoing,

Jesus loves you. Jesus loves you. Jesus loves you.

Sapling

My father thought he could cure his knee
by swinging his injured leg over the kitchen table.

I'd collect my dolls to watch from the doorway.
He's ruptured his cruciate ligament, I'd say,
as if I understood the words.

From there I could touch
the taper and curve of his wooden crutches,
propped against a wall like saplings,

could imagine my black crayon
had made grains in the ash-wood,
lines headed one way then the other – a pirate's map.

If my father caught me looking I'd flip my gaze into the garden,
to the beginnings of a plum tree, delicate in the sun.

It didn't draw me the way those crutches did.
Years later, that tree still stands. On visits home,
I'll settle on a blanketed lawn to sketch it,

adjust my pencil to suit the light, set the lines to be reborn.
I know this tree and its moods better than I knew my father.

Sometimes I'll think of his hands
gently planting the next-to-nothing of a sapling,
of his shadow where other shadows now fall.

It's as though I can see him.
A stranger picking plums.

In a Museum with Frida Kahlo

It comes to us all.
For me it came in a museum with Frida Kahlo
in the dead of night.

Shadows fell from her paintings,
slashed my pool of light.
Frida in chains, at play with a monkey, and in a hospital bed.

The groan of cooling walls accompanied me to the top floor.
I glimpsed Frida again in photographs –
her long neck strained, eyebrows arched, eyes dark as my own.

No star-filled sky or lure of Lisbon streets
could wrench me from Frida.
It was my son's voice. How he wasn't coming home.
Not then. Not for a long time.

It comes to us all. Missing children.
For me it came in a museum with Frida Kahlo
in the dead of night.

Sign Language

We share a bench among the wild-flower borders,
stinging with heat, the hiss of grasshopper all around.

She chats away in Japanese.
I sigh a glass-blower's sigh, make ready for silence.

Her perfect fingers begin to dance,
weaving silk from air. I follow, my hands scribbling.

Our gestures grow brighter, bolder.
They tell of tumbling sea otters, or is it the spooling of wool?

Of warblers carrying clouds on their backs,
a shore at low sun, its orangey glow, and the thrill of paddling.

Of cherry blossom, pink clustered parks,
the splash of Spring rain.

I think of bringing you to this garden
but could our damp words make it blaze?

As the moon rises over the old house,
stirred by Night Blooming Jasmine, I learn to say

sayounara.

Afterword

Touching Sharks in Monaco looks at memory and the distortion of memory – things remembered, things imagined. It addresses loss and trauma in family histories, the transience of nature, and ecological concerns. Further inspiration comes from a curiosity or need to make sense of myself and others, capturing both brief moments as I see them unfold around me and bigger moments from lived experience.

Touching Sharks In Monaco is Belinda Rimmer's first collection.

Indigo Dreams Publishing Ltd
24, Forest Houses
Cookworthy Moor
Halwill
Beaworthy
Devon
EX21 5UU
www.indigodreams.co.uk